DESTINATIONS

DESTINATIONS

A Photographer's Journey

ANDRÉ GALLANT

FOR CORNELIA & WES,
BEST WISHES
&
HAPPY TRAVELS,

André Gallant

AN ANDRÉ GALLANT BOOK

For your continuous support, the joy and laughter you bring
into my life, this book is dedicated to you, Parker.

National Library of Canada Cataloguing in Publication

Gallant, André
Destinations : a photographer's journey / André Gallant.

ISBN 0-9734714-1-7

1. Travel photography. I. Title.

TR790.G34 2005   778'.991   C2004-906647-1

Page 1: Smiling face, Portugal.
Page 2: Woman and her baby, Quito, Ecuador.
Page 5: Vine and flower against an old house, Portugal countryside.

CONTENTS

PREFACE 7

INTRODUCTION 12

SHRINE ON THE GANGES 14

PARAÍSO DEL SOL 34

GLIMPSES 56

ALASKA SYMPHONY 80

POUR LE PLAISIR DES YEUX 94

IDYLL PLEASURES 116

SERENE CANVASES 138

O CANADA 158

ABOUT TRAVEL PHOTOGRAPHY 184

Men in silhouette with a glimpse of the Taj Mahal through the mist.

PREFACE

I had just left Toronto, and I was already restless. I'd told my boss the train ride to Montreal would give me a chance to sort things out in my head, but the truth was I was afraid to fly. I'd just accepted a position managing a satellite stock photography office for the company that employed and represented me, the Image Bank. The goal of this trip was to find an office space and meet with some potential clients. My mind was racing, and I wasn't sure about my decision.

On the empty seat next to me lay a magazine called *Destinations,* a travel supplement to Canada's leading newspaper, *The Globe and Mail.* As I looked at the photographs, I thought to myself, "Wow, it must be nice to travel, take pictures and be paid for it." I put the magazine back on the seat and began to play out the week ahead in my mind. I couldn't help but feel this whole trip was a big mistake.

By the time I returned to Toronto, I'd decided to tell my boss I couldn't accept her job offer, that it didn't feel right, and that as hard as it was I wanted to make it as a photographer. My decision final, a huge weight was lifted off my shoulders. Now, it was time to start working on a travel portfolio.

I kept working at the Image Bank, mostly in the library, filing slides. Once I'd earned enough money, I took time off to travel and make photographs. I booked inexpensive last-minute trips to places such as Barbados, Jamaica and Costa Rica, and a cruise through the Greek islands. A year went by, and I felt ready. Portfolio in hand, I went to the offices of *Destinations.* I was asked to drop off my book for the day and pick it up after 4:00 p.m. When I returned to the office to pick up my slides, the receptionist informed me that the art director would be down in a few minutes. I nervously met Nadia, who told me she liked my work. She said, and I quote, "I want to send you somewhere. Call me back in a few weeks, and I may have something for you."

Exactly two weeks later, I nervously dialled the number and asked to speak to Nadia.

"I don't have very good news," she said. "I'm leaving the magazine."

Needless to say, I was devastated. Back to the Image Bank, for a while.

Months passed, and I heard of Nadia's replacement, Cate. I went through the process of dropping off my portfolio. Like déjà vu, Cate brought me my portfolio and told me she wanted to send me somewhere. She would call when she knew the magazine's new line-ups.

A week went by and no call. A month went by . . . two . . . three. Finally, six months later, I decided to call her.

"Hi, Cate, this is André Gallant calling."

"André, I was just about to call you. How would you like to go to Spain to shoot some gardens for us?"

It was the opportunity I'd been waiting for. I travelled to Barcelona, Aranjuez (near Madrid) and Seville in August. I was to photograph the gardens as art. What I was not prepared for was the heat that greeted me upon my arrival (the thermometer hovered around 45 degrees Celsius on most days). The gardens, although depleted of people and flowers, were nevertheless stunning. I did the shoot on slide film, except for a roll of black-and-white infrared film, which I'd been wanting to try out.

Photographs of Park Guell in Barcelona (designed by the famed architect Antoni Gaudi), the majestic trees and baroque statuary of Aranjuez and the tiled benches adorning Maria Luisa Park in Seville illustrated the story "Spanish Gardens: Shades of Green," and a shot of a lone park bench earned me my first cover. I was on my way.

Little did I know the impact the few infrared shots would have on the art director. Cate was very impressed with them, and I believe that led her to assign me to go to Portugal. The story would take me to the unspoiled northern countryside around Porto. The writer provided me with a shoot list that read something like this: Porto, Amarante, Coimbra and Bisalhaes (which is a small grouping of houses not even on a map). Also on the list was Douro, Portugal's wine-producing area, and Minho, a wilderness area where ponies roam wild. *Azulejos* (Portuguese tiles), cork trees and black pottery rounded up the list. My mission was to photograph as many places and items as possible. After landing in Lisbon, I rented a car and began driving north. I went to all the towns and villages on the list.

Although I'm not very religious, I was moved by Fatima and the weight of people's faith. I felt quite at ease aiming my camera at some of the pilgrims doing penance. I remember photographing a young girl lighting candles. As she heard the sound of the camera, she looked my way for an instant; again I released the shutter. I was very touched by people's kindness, and that made it easy for me to photograph them. The pace of the trip was relaxed, and I felt good about my photographs. When I took my Portugal shoot to *Destinations,* Cate informed me she was leaving the magazine.

In the interim, Jack McIver, the founder and editor of *Destinations* commissioned me to photograph the story of a group of people sailing through some islands off the coast of Maine. I was living in New Brunswick at the time, so, I drove to Camden, Maine, and embarked on my journey on the ninety-foot sailboat. The passengers, crew and I spent the next three days enjoying the sea, hopping from one island to the next.

Kelly Michelle stepped in as art director (number three for me) and laid out my Portugal shoot, "North to Bisalhaes." I earned my second cover with a photograph of a young boy taking a chicken to market in Porto.

Destinations went through major changes and began to be produced in-house at *The Globe and Mail,* with all-new staff. I dropped my portfolio at reception once again. As before, I met Karen when she brought me my slides and tear sheets. Although she liked my work, I sensed we had not really connected. Before I left, Karen asked if I had any photographs of Nevis. I didn't.

I felt a deep sense of disappointment. Walking back to a friend's place where I was staying, I had an idea and felt a rush of excitement come over me. Once I arrived at the apartment, I went to the phone and nervously dialled Karen's number. I asked her why she was looking for photographs of Nevis. *Destinations* was doing a story of the island, and they had decided to use stock images. I spontaneously offered to go to Nevis and shoot on spec for them (when you shoot on spec, you shoot photos on your own, with the possibility that a client will buy the rights to use them). It was a hard offer to refuse; Karen accepted it.

A month later I was off to the island of Nevis (the sister island to St. Kitts) with a shoot list in hand. With my savings, I booked a flight to St. Kitts, then took the ferry over to Nevis. I rented an economy car, found a small, inexpensive hotel and spent a week photographing the beauty of the island and, especially, its people. From dawn to dusk, I would circle the small island and photograph items and places on the author's list, but also things that appealed to me.

I felt I needed to photograph the people if I was to do the story and the island justice. I spent a lot of time getting to know the islanders before asking if I could photograph them. One man, who lived with his pet pig in a tiny house, appeared very lonely. Although he was the father of eight, his children did not visit much. I made a point of dropping by every day for a brief visit.

One day I asked an elegant elderly woman if I could take her portrait. She invited me into her house, and after a long and pleasant conversation, she asked if I could come back the next day, when she would have an answer for me. The next morning, a Sunday, I knocked on her door. She appeared with her hair pinned back, wearing a beautiful white dress with pink flowers. I asked again if I could photograph her. "I want to ask you a question before giving you an answer," she said. "Are you Catholic?" Pleased with my answer, she posed for me.

I took the shoot to the *Globe*'s offices, not really knowing what photographs they would use, if any. It was a huge gamble on my part, but it paid off. All the pictures they used to illustrate the article were mine, and a portrait of a young girl wearing a school uniform earned me my third cover. When I saw it in print, I thought to myself "Wow, I took those images!" Credit to a good art director: Karen did a great job. One of the spreads was made up of four photographs with predominant pink and blue hues. "Idyll Pleasures" received a National Magazine Award for photojournalism.

On a gloomy day in the middle of January 1992, I answered the phone: "André, where would you like to go on a shoot for us? Egypt, China or South America?" Stunned by Karen's offer, I chose to travel to the Siwa Oasis, in Egypt.

I arrived at the Cairo airport. I was not prepared for the mess and confusion. A stranger took me aside and led me through the massive crowd. Moments later, a customs officer stamped my passport. The stranger took my bags and led me outside to a taxi stand. I don't remember how much I tipped him, but whatever the amount, it was well worth it. I was in a hotel room in Cairo thirty minutes after having landed.

I spent a few days in Cairo before setting off on my assignment. From Cairo, I took a bus to Alexandria, where I stayed overnight. The next morning, I boarded another bus for the ten-hour ride to the Siwa Oasis, which borders Libya. The bus was crowded, and the air was laden with exhaust fumes. I felt extremely uncomfortable and isolated. For the first time, I wondered what the hell I was doing. When we finally arrived in the small village of Shali, I found a small hotel and booked a room, feeling tired and lonely. At two dollars a night, this was all the place was worth. It was so cold and dirty that I slept with my damp clothes on. The glamorous life of a travel photographer!

As it usually does, everything seemed better the next morning. The sun was warm, the sky was blue and the scenery was stunning. Shali is surrounded by 400,000 verdant date palms and fig trees, all in the middle of the Sahara Desert. As I walked the streets of the village, I noticed the scarcity of native woman, and later found out that recently wed woman are not allowed out of the house for a full year. I encountered mostly men and children. The kids would run up to me and ask for pens. Occasionally, I saw fully veiled women being rushed home by their husbands. I spent ten days in Siwa, capturing daily life, photographing at markets and taking portraits of men and children. A photograph of an old man walking up stairs that lead to a mosque graced the cover of *Destinations*. In predominant hues of gold and beige, the four double-page spreads that illustrated "Desert Calm" included photographs of the town of Shali, the Sahara, men and children and, yes, one of a veiled woman.

A few months later, Karen asked me to go to South America. Within a month, I was on my way to Ecuador. I landed in Quito and spent a few days there. It took me a while to get accustomed to the high altitude. I stayed in the old part of the city, its elegant architecture noticeable especially in its more than eighty churches.

I rented a car and replicated the writer's itinerary, which took me from Quito to Otavalo (famous for its weekly market), then all the way to Cuenca. I drove with trepidation through mist and clouds on the Avenue of the Volcanos. The scenery was absolutely stunning, with small villages dotting low-lying valleys and tropical forests where orchids sprout from the wet vegetation like dandelions through grass. It was the scariest drive of my life, and certainly the most dramatic. It was comforting to reach the pleasant city of Cuenca, but I knew I still had to drive back.

"The Florence of the Americas" was illustrated with images of old architecture, lavish church interiors, people dressed up in festive colours, and lush green valleys. A young boy laughing, his two front teeth missing, graced the cover.

My last assignment from Karen came in the form of a fax, asking me if I'd like to go to "Galicia, in Spain." Anticipating the cloudy weather (it's usual to have rain and clouds two out of three days in Galicia), and wanting to create a certain mood, I decided to photograph the assignment using high-speed grainy film (Agfachrome 1000). The route of many pilgrimages, Galicia is in the remote northern part of Spain.

Old bicycle against wall with hydrangeas, Portugal

As I expected, it was cloudy most of the time, and my choice of film was a good one. "To the Edge of the Earth" was nominated for a National Magazine Award for photography.

Karen eventually moved to New York and was replaced by George (art director number five), who assigned me two stories, one of the small village of Villa Canale in central Italy and the other of Quebec's Eastern Townships. Nominated for a National Magazine Award, the image of the Eastern Townships, which I photographed using the grainy film technique, became my last cover (number seven) and final contribution to *Destinations*, as *The Globe and Mail* decided to cease production of the award-winning magazine.

In a span of four years, with nine assignments taking me to eight countries over four continents, *Destinations* shaped my career as a travel photographer and played a very important role in my life, hence the title of this book.

Thank you to all who were involved.

André Gallant
December 2004

INTRODUCTION

Putting this book together has helped me revisit some favourite destinations and has brought back many wonderful memories. I came across a few images that evoked the kind of nostalgic emotion you sometimes feel when hearing certain songs or distinguishing certain smells. As I looked at thousands of slides, I reminisced over some of the images:

- *Three Greek men in front of a taverna, with raised glasses of ouzo.* What the picture does not tell is how, moments later, the men waved me over and started buying me rounds of the licorice-flavoured liquor. No word was spoken between us, but there was a lot of laughter and cheering.
- *A man pouring tea on his boat, Turkish flag batting in the wind.* I spent quite some time photographing "tea time" with this stranger. As if it were yesterday, I still remember how he waved goodbye as I was walking away.
- *Three woman laughing while working in a field in Portugal.* As I was leaving after photographing them, they intervened and poured me a glass of wine, and another, and another. All the time, we were communicating with our expressions.

Some images I photographed more than a decade ago affected me deeply when I viewed them anew. The photograph of a woman doing penance, advancing on her knees on the long path that leads to the church in Fatima, Portugal, made me wonder what she was praying for. Was she praying for herself or, perhaps, her children?

I came across a few architectural photographs of windows from some of the majestic old churches in Quito, Ecuador. Looking back at these, I can still recall the dampness inside the churches and the smell of burning incense. I also remember how the echo reverberated through these places of worship.

Other memories I'd rather forget also surfaced, such as the two times all my photography equipment was stolen, once from my hotel room in Rome while I was sleeping, and once from the trunk of my rental car in Cancun while I was swimming in the Caribbean. Then there was the time I was detained in Egypt and interrogated for four hours. The sign near the gate was written in Arabic, so how could I know I was riding my bike through a military compound, camera dangling from my neck, photo vest full of film? When I saw soldiers with bazookas on their shoulders, it was too late to turn back . . . These dreadful moments do make good stories, though.

When putting *Destinations* together, I wanted to share how I felt when travelling to some of my favourite countries, such as Morocco and Mexico, so I've added my memories to these photographs for the chapters "Pour le plaisir des yeux" and "Paraíso del sol."

Most recently I traveled to India. I was sick for most of that journey and disliked being there, but upon returning home, I wanted desperately to go back. How ironic. Having photographed my experiences in India, I needed to also put them into words, and did so in "Shrine on the Ganges."

"Glimpses" is just that: a quick peek into various countries, with a few images. "Serene Canvases" is made up of painting-like images captured in Europe. I hope the technique does these evocative places justice. "Idyll Pleasures" is a collection of colourful images of the Caribbean, some photographed when I was working on my portfolio and some shot on assignment. The focus of "Alaska Symphony" is of a grand landscape depleted of people.

I debated whether to include photos of Canada, and ultimately decided to do so. With "O Canada" I share some photographs made while working on the three books I illustrated for Pierre Berton: *Winter, The Great Lakes* and *Seacoasts.*

Finally, I share some notes in "About Travel Photography" that I hope will help you create your own wonderful memories.

Men at a tavern drinking ouzo.

SHRINE ON THE GANGES

A burning candle — an offering to the Ganges.

The cool breeze feels good on my face. The air is thick with fumes, but I can still distinguish certain smells: spices, burning wood and sewage. The combination is slightly nauseating. Raju manoeuvres the auto rickshaw through meandering alleyways with precision. The bumpy ride, which seems like a collision course, is just another fare for my hired driver.

We leave the rickshaw and walk the rest of the way. I fall behind Raju as there is so much to see. I also need to watch where I'm walking; the cows have been through here before us. We reach a corridor strewn with bodies wrapped in blankets—the homeless, still asleep. As we exit onto Kedar Ghat, the dawn colours are muted by the morning mist. It's as if I'm looking through a fine Indian silk fabric. Already,

boats with tourists cling to the shore, as onlookers watch the daily rituals. Unexpectedly, Raju comes over with hot tea. I appreciate the gesture and am glad for the warming beverage. The sun will soon be rising, and my boatman awaits me.

Located on the western banks of the Ganges, Varanasi, also known as Benares, is one of India's holiest places. The city has many nicknames: the Holy City, the city of light, the city of Shiva (one of Hindu's many gods, often represented with snakes around his neck and a third eye symbolizing wisdom). Rituals of life and death take place everyday on the famous ghats (steps) that lead to the river. With a population of more than 2 million people, Varanasi is crowded and polluted. A visit to the Ganges is nevertheless an amazing experience that will affect you for the rest of your life.

My journey on the river begins. The sun is rising, bathing in warm light the people that have come to the sacred river. Men in dhotis and women in colourful saris perform rituals of prayer, chanting as the river washes away their sins. A private display made public. I notice a group of Buddhist monks coming down to the river, their saffron-and-crimson robes brilliant against the white-and-orange steps. Reluctantly, I begin to photograph as my journalistic instincts take over.

Lalu, my boatsman, rows slowly upstream. He's very attentive, and pauses when I take photographs. The father of five children, he's been doing this for twenty years. We go by Prabuh Ghat, where people are washing sheets and laying them to dry on the steps. When we reach Asi Ghat, the southernmost ghat, where the Asi River meets the Ganges, we turn around and begin floating downstream. It's getting warmer, and more people appear on the steps. Children begin to play cricket, small kites appear in the sky, and vendors descend upon tourists, selling everything from postcards to body massages.

We pass Kedar Ghat, our starting point, and continue downstream. Dasashvamedh Ghat, one of Varanasi's holiest spots, is bustling with people. Priests, sitting under parasols, pray with the pilgrims who flock to the Holy City. The steps are full of people, some praying and offering flowers and incense to the river, others washing and brushing their teeth. To my amazement, some are drinking the water.

As we near Manikarnika Ghat, I see smoke rising from the funeral pyres. This is the largest of the two famed cremation ghats. The piles of wood scattered everywhere are haunting. A group of men descends on the river, carrying a body swathed in colourful gold cloth on a bamboo stretcher. The corpse is doused one last time in the river before the cremation. No less than six fires are going. Some people are singing and dancing to the sound of a few drums.

My eyes go back to the smoking pyres. I feel extremely uneasy but am compelled to watch. In one of the raging fires I notice two protruding limbs. We proceed downriver.

The larger of the two crematoriums in Varanasi, Manikarnika Ghat is considered by Hindus an auspicious place to be cremated or, to come to die. Fires burn day and night as people are cremated and the ashes are offered to the Ganges. The cremation takes about three hours and costs 300 rupees (less than ten dollars Canadian). Deemed pure, children under twelve and pregnant woman are not cremated. Their bodies are wrapped, weighed down and offered to the river.

I observe a man sitting cross-legged on the steps, in deep meditation. He wears his hair long, and he's dressed in shiny fabrics in hues of gold and silver. "That is holy man," says Lalu.

We pass by Scindia Ghat, where years ago a temple to Shiva fell. It lies there still, partially submerged in the river. Something floating in the river catches my eye. I'm relieved to see it's an animal, a dead bull, no doubt an offering to the river.

As we approach Panchaganga Ghat, I see a group of woman standing in a circle. In the middle stands a priest, a stretcher at his feet. The body is wrapped in fabric, but the face of an elderly woman is exposed. As the women pray and wail, a phone rings. Bemused, I look in the direction of the sound and see no less than three men talking on their cell phones. Thousands of years of tradition meets the wave of the future.

We reach the last and northernmost ghat, the Adi Kesheva, and turn around once more to return to Kedar Ghat, where Raju is waiting to take me back to my hotel. One last chance to admire the shrines and temples that line the river and to steal a final look at its worshippers. I feel privileged to have witnessed their spirituality. The Taj Mahal may be the pride of India, but Varanasi is without a doubt its soul.

Opposite: Tourists on the Ganges at sunrise.

Above: One of the many shrines along the ghats at Varanasi.

Opposite: Buddhist monks on the steps of Kedar Ghat.

Above and opposite: Men and women come here to pray and bathe. How fortunate I was to witness such a beautiful ritual.

A young boy brings tea to some of the worshippers.

Bathed in warm sunlight, this woman, unaffected by my presence, goes about her ritual.

Above and opposite: The Ganges in the late afternoon light. Young boys come down to the ghats to play ball and fly kites.

Following pages: Women and men lay out sheets and clothes to dry by the river at Prabuh Ghat.

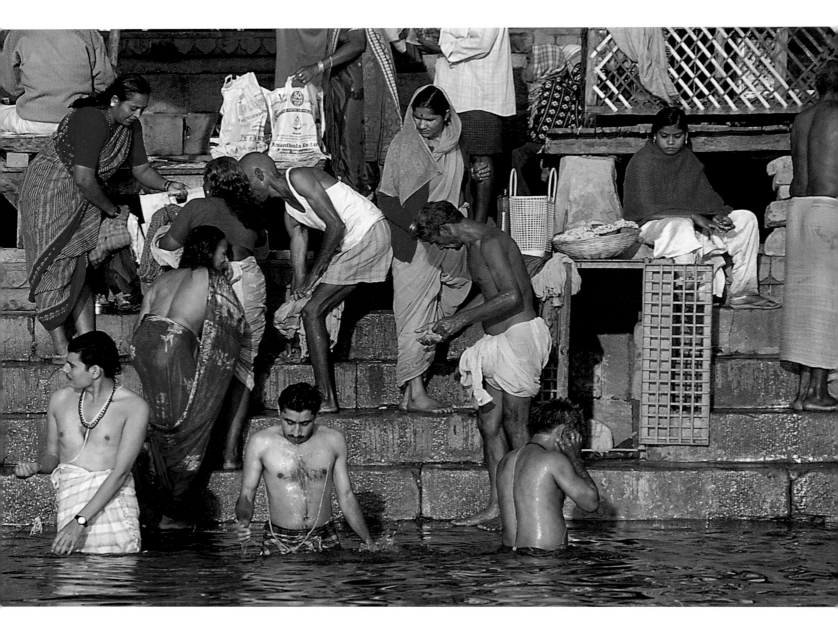

Above and opposite: People come to the river to pray, meditate and wash.

Following pages: Early morning rituals of prayer.

Above: Colourful boats on the Ganges.

Opposite: My boatsman Lalu has been working on the Ganges for the past twenty years.

PARAISO DEL SOL

Bell tower, Izamal, Mexico.

"You're going around in circles; it's a roundabout!" says Parker.

"I know," I snap back. "I don't know where to exit, and I don't have time to read the signs. Do you want to drive?"

The traffic is hectic, and I find the city of Mérida very confusing. Parker and I have spent over an hour looking for a road that will lead us out of the city, and the tension is thick between navigator and driver. I somehow, by chance, end up on the *periférico* (a highway that surrounds some Mexico cities). As the traffic subsides, our breathing slows down and we begin to laugh at ourselves. We've finally made it out of Mérida, and we're both hungry.

Two small tables with a few plastic chairs are set up by the highway. "Do you want to try it?" I ask Parker. We both like to eat at small places, places the locals frequent. As always, I curse myself for not having learned Spanish. I know *pollo con papas,* and order for both of us, with *dos cokas.* The woman informs me there are no potatoes, but they have *sopa* of something I can't understand. We both order soup and wait to see what kind it is.

We're still chuckling over the driving incident as we watch the señorita put our chicken on the grill. She goes into her house and comes back with two Cokes and the soup. "How is it?" I ask Parker, the more daring of us when it comes to food. "Really tasty," he says. And it is. Noodles, chicken livers and a very nice broth. Then comes the grilled chicken with cabbage salad and tortillas. The emaciated family dog lies down beside us. As we devour our chicken, we watch children running through the house. We pay for our meal with disbelief: it costs only 34 pesos (about $3.50).

Back on the road, on our way to the Hacienda San José, my back aches from the driving and the stress. When we finally arrive at our destination, my shirt is so wet it clings to my body.

We are greeted by the manager, and the bellhop brings us cold towels and fruit juice. This is why we have come here: for the small details that make us feel like guests rather than numbers. We're shown our room and the grounds of the hacienda. The garden is beautiful, set against a backdrop of colourful structures that make up the rooms and suites, the restaurant and an on-site chapel. Large trees grace the land, along with agave plants and bougainvillea in various colours. I notice a pond with water lilies, my favourite, in the deepest shade of burgundy. The manager informs us we'll be dining in the garden tonight. Finally we can relax and enjoy this paradise. It is time for a swim.

Parker and I get up early to photograph the next morning. The sun is just coming up, burning the thin mist that hovers above the ground, and the light is glorious on the garden. We have the place to ourselves. The red bougainvillea stands stark against the walls, painted a shade deeper than periwinkle. A small pond has painted daisies floating around, and to my surprise, the water lilies are out this early in the morning. The garden is tranquil; all we can hear are the songs of a few birds. Parker and I meet up for breakfast and plan the day ahead of us. We'll be leaving soon to drive to the next hacienda.

The two-hour drive to Hacienda Temozón takes us a leisurely six hours. We take the long way there, stopping occasionally to take photographs. Most villages, no matter how small, have at least a main square with a small church, and we stop at every one of them. I'm really taken by the colours of these places of worship. Yellow appears to be the most common, but I also photograph *iglesias* in hues of pink, red and green.

We drive through towns with names like Teco, Mani and Mama. As we exit the small village of Tekit, I notice to the left of the road a dilapidated fence enclosing a small graveyard. I must take a look. The cemetery is filled with bone repositories inscribed with the names of the deceased and dates. A few candles — from the previous evening, I assume — are burning. The door of one of the repositories is ajar, showing its contents. A human skull appears to be standing guard. I find this both eerie and fascinating. Although I feel it's an intrusion, I'm compelled to photograph it. I spend an hour capturing on film some of these colourful displays. I sense Parker's uneasiness and reluctantly decide to leave. This site remains imprinted in my mind for the rest of the day.

We arrive in the middle of the afternoon. Hacienda Temozón (which means "whirlwind") is more than three hundred years old. At one time, this area of Mexico was a leading producer of sisal (a fibre made from the henequen plant). In the late 1950s, the demand for sisal waned, and many haciendas were abandoned. Temozón has been reborn as a boutique hotel, with seventeen rooms and eleven suites.

After settling in our room, we explore the grounds with our cameras. I spend a good amount of time chasing after a peacock, its feathers in full display. Once the colourful bird stops showing off, I join Parker for a swim in the pool. We spend the rest of the day lounging around and relaxing. Tomorrow we're driving to Uxmal.

We set off late in the morning, lingering as long as we can to enjoy the hacienda. We travel through small villages in search of churches and cemeteries. In Ticul we find a large graveyard, ablaze with colour, containing old tombstones in a state of decay and more recent ones lacking character. Fresh gladiolas are propped against crosses, while plastic flowers, their hues faded from the sun, grace the smaller gravestones. Larger monuments are decorated with tiles of intricate design in a melange of colours. We spend an hour photographing and wandering the small clustered alleys.

Hunger informs us it's way past lunchtime. We go to a small Italian restaurant in town and order pizza, a Corona for Parker and a glass of white wine for me. Our server, a man in his late sixties who is very likely the owner, brings us the *cerveza y vino blanco*. He struggles to pull out the cork from the half-full bottle of wine. In a move of desperation, he tries to pull it out with his few remaining teeth. Parker and I are careful not to look at each other and manage to keep our composure, at least for a few minutes. We both get a good laugh out of it, and Parker, who's in the restaurant business, leaves a hefty tip.

We reach Uxmal later that afternoon. As both of us are tired, we decide to visit the Mayan site the next morning.

After breakfast, we wander over to the gates at Uxmal. We pay the entry fee and proceed inside to the ruins. Standing majestically tall in front of us is the Pyramid of the Magician (la Pirámide del Adivino), built on an oval base. We climb to the top, and we're immediately transported back in time. In front of us we can see the entire layout of the site, now surrounded by jungle.

We walk over to the next large complex, the Nunnery Quadrangle (el Cuadrangulo de las Monjas). The four temples that form the quadrangle face a large courtyard. The Chac masks and serpents that decorate the structures are very impressive, and they photograph well.

We head next to the Governor's Palace (el Palacio del Gobernador), an exquisite, magnificent structure. Upon close inspection of the facade, also festooned with Chac faces, we notice in the cracks large iguanas basking in the sun. Adjoining the palace are the Great Pyramid (Gran Pirámide), the South Temple (el Templo del Sur) and the Pigeon House (el Palomar). Many smaller structures are scattered around the site, but the heat is getting the better of us. We agree to leave, but I must stop by the Nunnery Quadrangle and the Pyramid of the Magician for one final view. Reluctantly, we exit the gates of Uxmal.

We drive south to Hacienda Uayamón (*Uayamón*

means "Here we go"), in the state of Campeche. In the sixteenth century, this hacienda was a cattle ranch. Its history holds tales of ravage by English pirates. Now it is a beautiful hotel. Surrounded by exuberant foliage, the rooms appear to be in the middle of the jungle. Near the main house stands a large *ceiba* (the sacred trees of the Mayas) more than one hundred years old. The grounds are well tended but not overly manicured. Old concrete walls surround the pool, in which two ancient columns stand erect. This is where we'll spend the rest of the day.

After dinner that evening, as we walk back to the room, we notice tree frogs at the base of the trees lining the path. These amphibians with large eyes and camouflaged bodies feed on the insects lured by the warm, bright lights. I want to photograph them, but I have only slow film and no flash; it will have to wait until morning.

Excited, I'm up before sunrise. Grabbing my camera gear and tripod, I rush outside to look for the frogs. I can't find them. I look carefully on the bark; I search in the dried leaves at the base of the trunks near the lights. No frogs. Disappointed, I return to the room. Parker is up, and I tell him I can't find the frogs. He watches nature shows and *Animal Planet*: he informs me the frogs are nocturnal. I sense a bit of sarcasm in his voice. I tell him I've looked everywhere for them — where could they be hiding? He adds, "They're tree frogs." Again, I detect that tone . . .

I go into the washroom to freshen up. I look in the trash can, and right there, staring at me, is a tree frog! We take the frog outside and set it free on one of the trees. Stunned, perhaps by the sunlight, it stays on the bark, motionless. I grab my camera and start to shoot. For a split second, the frog turns and stares at me. I click the shutter one last time before it climbs up the tree and disappears.

After breakfast, we depart for the Hacienda Santa Rosa, where we'll spend our last night in Mexico. We drive north, heading back to the Yucatan. Our map, although not very detailed, serves its purpose. Again we go through small villages, slowing down considerably for the abundant *topes* (speed bumps) lining the streets. This is rural Mexico. We stop a few times to take photos, and then it is lunchtime.

We drive past a few craft stalls with hammocks of all colours blowing in the wind and see a tiny restaurant with a large Dos Equis sign. We decide to try it. We order *sopa de lima* (lime soup, and it's wonderful) and, of course, *pollo con papas*. Before leaving, we buy a hammock as a souvenir.

We arrive at Hacienda Santa Rosa fairly early and settle into our room. The pool is just outside our door, and Parker goes for a swim. I would rather take photographs, and I decide to shoot some still lifes. The exterior of the hacienda is painted blue with white accents. I move a few wrought-iron chairs and a table closer to one of the walls and run into the room to get a glass vase with flowers that's on one of the dressers.

I begin to photograph different setups. I have brought with me on this trip an old Polaroid SX70, so I can do some Pola-painting (you can alter the look of this type of instant film by scratching the surface

of the Polaroid as the image gradually appears). I take a few shots and proceed to scratch and draw on the four-by-five-inch photos. I end up with a few that I really like.

Before dinner, Parker and I drive to a small bright yellow church nearby that we both noticed on the way in. The sun is near the horizon, so the light is soft and warm. We both begin to photograph. Parker shows me one of his compositions, a close-up of the yellow steeple with the date, 1906, carved into the concrete. A young boy watches our every move. I point to the camera, then point to him. A large smile appears on his face, and I take a few photographs of him. Moments later, the sun is gone.

We drive back to the hacienda before it is fully dark. It's been a wonderful trip, and I promise myself that I will learn a few more Spanish words for next time.

Opposite: Blue door on colourful house, Tecoh, Yucatan.

Top left: Lilies and gladioli in glass vase, Hacienda San José. Top right and bottom left: Painted walls, San Miguel de Allende. Bottom right: Potted geranium on small balcony, Queretaro.

Opposite: Moorish arches in courtyard, Art and Culture Centre, Queretaro.

Chairs and tables in the courtyard of a hacienda in Chichén Itzá.

Top left: Palm shadows in pool at the Hacienda San José. Top right: Tree frog at Hacienda Uayamón.
Bottom left: Palm fronds, Hacienda Temozón. Bottom right: Painted daisies in pool of water, Hacienda San José.

Wrought iron fence detail, Art and Culture Centre, Queretaro.

Opposite: Portrait of artist Didier Mayes, Oaxaca.

Top: Waiter at the
Hacienda San José.
Below: Staff folding
towels at pool side,
Hacienda Uayamón.

Opposite:
Bougainvillea in glass
vase at Hacienda
Santa Rosa.

Above: Boy covered with tar, in a pre-carnival ritual in San Martín Tilcajete, Oaxaca.

Opposite: Turkey lady at the market in Tlacolula.

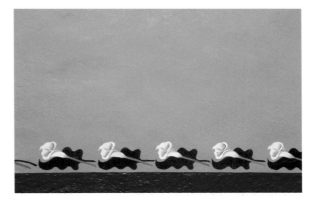

Above: Orange wall with painted calla lilies, San Miguel de Allende.

Opposite: Man selling cyclamen in San Miguel de Allende.

Watering the garden at Hacienda San José.

Intimate details of Hacienda San José. Top left: Bougainvillea and arches. Top right: Peacock showing off. Bottom left: Fronds against a blue wall. Bottom right: Exotic flowers near a villa.

I chose to photograph the Mayan ruins with black-and-white film (Kodak T400 CN), and asked the lab to sepia-tone the prints. I felt this added an old look to the images of these structures from the past.

Above: Upon close inspection of the ruins, iguanas appear in some cracks and crevices.

Opposite: The Governor's Palace at Uxmal with a view of the Grand Pyramid.

GLIMPSES

Detail of Pont Alexandre III and glimpse of la Tour Eiffel, Paris.

Through my years of travelling, some places have inspired photographs that are important to me for personal reasons. In this chapter, I share these images with you; the captions divulge what I was thinking when I took them, or what has made them important to me since then.

Opposite: Mist in a field of tulips, Sassenheim, Netherlands.

Fatima, Portugal

When on assignment in Portugal, I came to
Fatima, where in 1917 the blessed Virgin Mary
appeared six times to three children. I was taken
by the weight of people's faith at this famous
pilgrimage site. I photographed an older woman
doing penance, advancing towards the church on
her knees. She appeared to be in a trance and was
oblivious to my presence. I wondered what she
was praying for, or for whom. Later that day I
saw this young girl lighting candles. I wondered
if someday she'd come back to this place and
offer a similar sacrifice.

Costa Rica

These architectural details of a church in Costa Rica helped me land my first travel assignment for *Destinations*. When asking me to photograph "Spanish Gardens," Cate, the art director, wanted me to shoot the gardens as art, like the pictures of the green church she'd seen in my portfolio six months earlier.

Istanbul, Turkey

Crowded and colourful, Istanbul is fascinating and exotic. As we approached the city from the water, the smog was so thick it robbed the sprawling city of all its colour. The mosques stood out above the skyline, appearing as silhouettes. The harbour, alive with fishermen selling the day's catch, was a foreign site, but the smell was familiar to me. The souks were full of people haggling and buying. Stacks of Turkish rugs created mosaic designs. The smell of leather permeated the air. There was much confusion and commotion. The Blue Mosque offered refuge from the heat, the noise and the crowds. For the first time in my life, I heard the almost haunting amplified call to prayer. I ended up back at the harbour, where I was the most comfortable. In the distance, a man on his boat was drinking tea, and I photographed the ritual. As I left, he waved goodbye. I waved back, a smile on my face.

New Zealand

I admire people who want to preserve their heritage, be they the Acadians in eastern Canada, the Inuit in the north or the Maori in New Zealand. A good friend in Pokekohe arranged for me to photograph a Maori adorned with *ta moko*. With the light coming from a window, I emphasized the tattoo by shooting up close and posing a profile. I used the same thought process when photographing a wood carving from a ceremonial house in Gisborne, on the North Island.

Cartagena, Colombia

In Cartagena, Colombia, I spent a day in the old part of the city. I wanted to photograph the cathedral, and I wanted to show scale and have a human element in the final image. By chance, this man walked past, providing both. The portrait of the man smiling was very spontaneous. When I saw him, I felt he had a lot of character, and I loved the hat. I pointed first to my camera, then to him. He broke into this beautiful smile, pride on his face, as his friends watched him being photographed.

Namibia

Namibia is a beautiful country, and one I caught only a glimpse of. It's a country I want to return to, so I can discover places I've only heard about — like the skeleton coast or Itosha — and revisit one of my favourite sites, Sossusvlei, in the Namib desert. The image on the left was taken at the entrance of Sossusvlei. The photo of the boy (above) was made in a tiny village in the south of Namibia.

Tuscany, Italy

It was May when I travelled to Tuscany to photograph the countryside. I fell in love with the verdant pastures, poppy fields and beautiful trees. I never made it to Florence or Sienna. I was so compelled by nature, I could not part with it. These were all photographed in central Tuscany as I travelled small roads passing through towns such as Pienza, Montepulciano and Buonconvento.

When I was on assignment for *Destinations* in Ecuador, these churches provided a refuge from the heat. Looking at these images, I recall the coolness inside, the fragrance of burning incense and the reverberating echo. The two photographs above are from the cathedral in Cuenca. The image on the right is from the Iglesia del Sagrario in Quito.

Greek Islands

My first visit to the Greek islands was on a cruise ship with a ridiculous itinerary that allowed passengers six hours on Mykonos and two hours on Santorini. I had to go back and do it my way. This time, I savoured the islands, which were bathed in warm light. I also discovered the crosses.

The Greek islands are populated with friendly people. I encountered many
with faces full of character. Most agreed to pose for me.

Siwa, Egypt

Remote and exotic, the oasis of Siwa seems like a mirage, surrounded by thousands of fig trees and the golden sand of the Sahara Desert. In the town of Shali, this young girl dressed in a shiny, colourful outfit and her two siblings stopped briefly, long enough to pose for me.

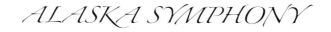

ALASKA SYMPHONY

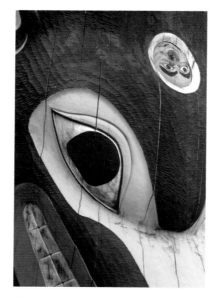

Totem pole detail, Petersburg, Alaska.

After many delays and a cancelled flight, I arrive in Juneau, Alaska, a day late. Everyone else is here, and I'm getting excited. I join Bob from California, Matt from Boston, Maria from Philadelphia, Dave from Victoria, Brian and Karen from Toronto and Danny from Israel. Danny received his visa just two days earlier. I have organized the trip — many months in the planning — with Tom and Jenn, owners of the

Oceanlight 2, a beautiful, seventy-one-foot sailboat. Their six-year-old daughter, Sarah, is also part of our group. We've come to photograph southeast Alaska in June, the driest month, sailing from Juneau to Prince Rupert, British Columbia. The ten-day journey will take us through Alaskan wilderness, visiting unspoiled beaches, fjords and icebergs. We're also hoping to see whales and bald eagles.

ADAGIO

Day 1: Overcast. After we load our gear on board, I assign everyone their cabins. Most of us have to share quarters, except for Bob, who makes sure I know that he's the senior in our group, and Dave, who confesses to heavy snoring. I fall for both excuses, and they get the two single cabins. Our journey begins. We depart Juneau at nine in the morning, on time. From the cockpit, we watch Tom navigate and, for the next four hours, admire the scenery as we head towards Wood Spit Island.

We land by zodiac, laden with cameras, tripods and other gear and wearing rubber boots, and spend the afternoon photographing. The grey clouds add a solemn mood to the seascapes. Several bald eagles that nest on the island fly above us, carrying their catch. They are wonderful to watch, but difficult to capture well on film. The wind picks up, so we head back to the boat and motor to Sanford Cove for the night. After a great meal, we tell stories, share laughter and watch Karen and Sarah sing and dance to the Proclaimers. The individuals begin to form a group.

Day 2: Rain, heavy at times. We stand in awe as we enter Ford's Terror, a cove so named because of strong currents created by the changing tides. Rain saturates the rich greens of the mountains. The sound of many waterfalls is hypnotic. Mist clings to the cliffs, and trees seem to spring out of the escarpment. We are captivated by the isolation and mesmerized by the grandeur of this landscape. Hampered by heavy rain,

we go ashore—we all feel the need to photograph the rising mist, flowing water, harlequin ducks and giant pond lilies. We shoot until the rain and dampness force us to quit.

Leaving the Terror behind, we motor through Andicot Arms, a large channel filled with icebergs. These towering sculptures, in hues from cerulean to azure, stand stark and magnificent against the grey sky. The inclement weather provides the right atmosphere for our photographs.

ANDANTE

Day 3: Cloudy. We enter Tracy Arm, another large channel littered with icebergs. The water is calm and a thick layer of mist hovers over the mountains. The first icebergs seem surreal against the grey sea and sky. Our shutters begin to click. Tom steers the boat towards the ice and circles the bergs until we are all satisfied. The sky brightens, but the sun stays hidden. It doesn't really matter.

We come upon a huge mass of ice. I suggest that someone go out in a kayak to add scale to the scenery. A few minutes later, Jenn, a former Canadian team synchronized swimmer, is paddling in front of the huge blue backdrop. She's dressed in red and yellow, the kayak's colours. The human element gives a whole new dimension to our images. We find a beach where we can go ashore and use our tripods. It's perfect for shooting abstracts of the ice and a really nice change to be able to steady our cameras and shoot at f/22.

Another grand day, topped off with a delicious dinner, a few bottles of wine and a lot of good conversation. I have yet to read a paragraph from the two books I brought along with me.

Day 4: Partly sunny. I wake to shrieks of excitement from Karen, and rush from my cabin and up onto the deck. A humpback whale breaches in the distance. I'm filled with amazement as it leaps from the sea. A crashing sound reaches us moments after it re-enters its own element. This is the Alaska we have come to see.

We motor through Frederick Sound to Baird Glacier, seeing whales, bald eagles and seals en route. Everything around us is so beautiful, right down to the simple rhythmic wake of the boat. We spend the night in a protected cove at Baird Glacier. The clouds have moved in again.

Day 5: Cloudy. We decide to go to the tiny community of Petersburg today to photograph the icebergs nearby. It's an opportunity to get off the boat for a while and to spend some time alone — just what we need. A good walk and a latte sound mighty good. For dinner, we feast on Alaskan crab legs that Tom bought from a fisherman earlier in the day. That's about as fresh as it gets.

LEGATO
Day 6: Cloudy, chance of clearing. We spend part of the morning in Petersburg. I sit beside two Tlingit totem poles, admiring the haunting carvings. I have always had an affinity for native art, and I study the bear, the raven and the thunderbird before going back to the sailboat. We head out to LeConte Bay Glacier, which was dormant until 1995. It is warm, and we are all overdressed. The sea is choppy so, instead of going all the way up to the glacier, we go ashore to photograph at the entrance to the bay, spending an hour or so shooting the rocks, the striations in the escarpment and small pools of water.

Blue patches begin to appear in the sky. We return to the zodiac and circle the scattered icebergs. The light intensifies; the wind drops; the water becomes still. We have difficulty containing ourselves and click our cameras in a frenzy. Our film stock gets low. I ask Tom to go around once again so we can get more pictures. We all crouch when Brian aims with his panoramic Hasselblad Xpan, fitted with a wide-angle lens. Finally, we agree that we've shot enough and are ready to abandon the bliss. Then the sun comes out — and we start all over again. As I hear the sound of film rewinding, I feel content. Everyone is having a wonderful time.

We return to the *Oceanlight 2* satiated: 124 rolls of film and more than 4,460 slides in four hours.

Back in Petersburg, Karen and Tom fish for herring to lure bald eagles. As they throw the fish into the water, the birds swoop, claws open, grabbing what they can. Everyone is photographing. It's quite a spectacle. The light is dim, and I'm panning at an eighth of a second with Velvia (colour reversal film). I'm dubious about the results, but it's worth a try. What a day this has been!

Day 7: Cloudy. We head south from Petersburg and travel for most of the day, passing the time reading or sitting on deck chatting and watching for whales. Sarah keeps us entertained by singing along to Pink as she listens to Matt's MP3 player. Finally, we anchor and it's time for a glass of wine.

ALLEGRISSIMO

Day 8: Cloudy. Winds to fifteen knots. Weighing anchor, we head south toward Ketchikan. The wind increases, and our speed decreases. The *Oceanlight 2* starts to bob up and down. Water flows into the open hatches — lots of water. We rush to close them, struggling to stay upright. As the wind howls and the waves swell, I make my way to the cockpit and notice that everyone is drained of colour. We huddle together, worry unmistakable in our eyes. The gusts increase to forty-four knots. So much for the forecast fifteen knots. We're all very quiet.

Our boat inches forward, and Tom asks Jenn to watch out for stranded logs. I get a knot in my stomach when I see one on our left. Tom's eyes meet mine. He sees it too, and knows all too well the threat it poses to the sailboat. I look at Maria; she is concentrating and appears very focused, but I worry: I had assured her that this trip would be smooth sailing. I also watch Brian — I know he is prone to seasickness. Although I haven't seen the movie or read the book, I feel as if we're living *The Perfect Storm.*

Thirty miles and seven hours later, we gratefully enter the small, calm cove of Meyers Chuck. The climax of our symphony, this day will certainly be the most unforgettable.

CODA

Day 9: Partly sunny. From Meyers Chuck we hoist the sails and head south. Once the wind catches the sail, our speed increases, the boat angles sideways, and we feel the powerful thrust. It is quite exciting for those of us not used to sailing. We're on the water for most of the day. We reach Pearl Harbor Beach early in the evening, drop anchor, and witness a dramatic sunset, with lenticular clouds catching the last rays of glowing light.

Day 10: Cloudy. We reach Prince Rupert, our final destination. Everyone's a bit sad that the trip is almost over, and we agree to have dinner aboard the *Oceanlight 2.* Jenn prepares another sumptuous meal. We toast her and Tom, our captain. Karen and Sarah have a last dance as the Proclaimers sing "And I will walk 500 miles, and I will walk 500 more . . ."

We are going back to reality. I feel especially for Danny, returning to the instability of his country, yet I know he's going home to a loving family. We all hug and kiss each other at the airport. Maria murmurs in my ear, "You changed my life!"

Above: I photographed this eagle in flight in Petersburg. Because of the low light, I was forced to pan the photograph, shooting at 1/8 of a second. The majestic bird was swooping down to catch the herring we were throwing into the water.

Opposite: The mist rises above the mountain on a wet day in Ford's Terror.

Above: Iceberg detail in LeConte Bay.

Opposite: After an amazing afternoon of photography at LeConte Bay, we were heading back to the sailboat when the dramatic sky opened up briefly, just long enough for us to photograph a few frames of this amazing light on the icebergs.

Above: I was quite taken by the beautiful and graphic wake of our boat.

Opposite: Islands in the mist, Frederick Sound.

Cascading mountains in the mist.

An iceberg in many shades of blue drifts slowly on Endicott Arm.

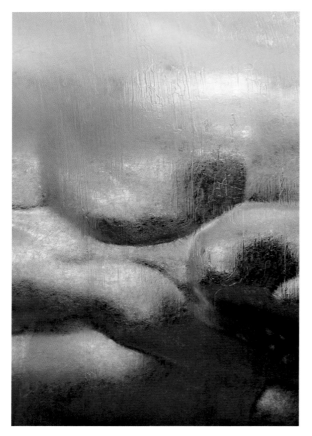

Above: A few icebergs were beached at Tracy Arm.
At last we were able to photograph these large masses
of ice, using our tripods. The photograph above is a
close-up of the ice.

Opposite: Jenn got into a kayak so we could have scale,
colour contrast and a human figure in our photographs.

POUR LE PLAISIR DES YEUX

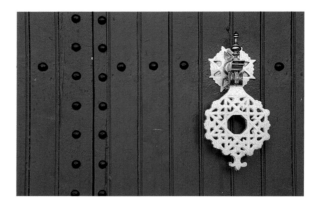

Door detail, Marrakech.

The sun is near the horizon. The warm light intensifies the ochre-coloured boulders scattered along the dramatic landscape. I finally reach Tafraoute, hidden in the Anti-Atlas mountains. Before securing a room for the night, I drive around looking for something to photograph, because this light is so glorious. I also want to familiarize myself with the area so I'll have an idea where I'd like to be at sunrise tomorrow. The high mountains obscure most of the light, and large portions of scenery fall into shade. I drive by a small village that appears cartoonish against a backdrop of towering cliffs. Oumesnat is where I want to be in the morning, as the mountains opposite it have claimed today's light.

After finding a hotel room, I step out into the night. A young man dressed in blue, wearing a black turban, steps out of nowhere. "Come see my shop," he says.

I politely decline his invitation: "I'm not interested in buying anything."

"Pour le plaisir des yeux" (for the pleasure of the eyes), he insists.

I walk into his shop. It looks like all the other ones I've been in before. Stacks of rugs along the walls, displays of antiqued daggers and jewellery. A friend, co-worker or both comes in with mint tea. I listen and watch as Brahim unfolds carpets of all sizes and colours. I keep thinking, I'm not buying any, I'm not buying any. I make the mistake of asking the price of the largest *kilim*.

As Brahim wraps my purchases, he asks where I'm off to next.

"The Sahara. I should be there in a few days," I say.

"I have a cousin in Erfoud," Brahim boasts. "He could take you there."

I thank him but say, "I'll manage."

Before leaving, I get an invitation to this man's wedding, which takes place the next month. I'm honoured but must decline. I put my two new rugs in the trunk of the car and go for dinner.

I reach Ouarzazate very late the next day. Too many photography stops! The city appears new except for the Taourirt Kasbah (kasbahs are fortified castles or prominent family dwellings), which lies on the edge of the city. The mud walls decorated with geometric patterns are very impressive. I notice a stork nesting in one of the towers. I opt to come here in the morning, when the sun will be in a better position. I find a hotel on the outskirts of town that doubles as a movie set/studio. Before dinner, I wander around some of the shops. I'm offered everything from rugs to beautiful pottery produced in Safi. Before I leave the shop empty-handed, I'm offered a Berber massage. I certainly don't want one of those . . .

I'm off before sunrise, with a stop at the Taourirt Kasbah. I spend the next hour or so photographing as the sunlight paints life onto the mud-plastered walls. With the long drive ahead, I must go now if I want to reach the Sahara before the sun sets. As I leave the mountains behind, the landscape opens up. The terrain becomes arid, except for the occasional oasis sprouting along the Dades valley. Separated by long stretches of road, the towns I drive through are alive and colourful by comparison. The driving is consuming my time, and I fight the urge to stop to take pictures. The desert beckons.

I finally reach Erfoud, the last town before the desert. I near a petrol station and some children approach my car. They are shouting my name! "André, André . . ." They touch the car and lead me somewhere. I follow them to a small café. A man sitting at one of the tables comes over and introduces himself. "Bonjour, André, my name is Isham. I am Brahim's cousin, and I'll take you to the desert."

After I fill up the car with petrol, Isham takes over as the driver, and we head for the Sahara. It's a difficult drive in a small car. I'm relieved to have a guide and driver. We speed east on a terrible paved road, which gives way to a dirt road that eventually disappears. All that is left are tire tracks that criss-cross through gravel and patches of sand. Half an hour later, the dunes of Erg Chebbi appear in the distance. We're still half an hour away, Isham informs me. I get excited and anxious at the same time. The imagery is surreal, with the sand dunes beginning abruptly, like the waves of an ocean. We approach the towering mountains of sand sculpted by the wind. The light plays games, contouring these towering mountains of sand with highlights and shadows, swapping them mornings and evenings.

There are a few *auberges* along the dunes. Isham has arranged a room at Auberge Erg Chebbi. My driver will spend the night and bring me back to Erfoud the next day. Tripod in hand and camera around my neck, I embark on my journey into the desert. I fervently climb the dunes, leaving tracks behind. I'm hoping to find dunes that have not been trampled by anyone. As I head farther into the Sahara, the dunes, devoid of footprints, appear pristine. I'm moved by this sea of sand; it must be the Pisces in me. The colour of the sand deepens as the sun nears the horizon. I fight the urge to climb higher, always wanting to see beyond the next dune. I'm delighted to be here, and I take many photographs.

As soon as the sun sets behind the mountains, I feel a chill in the air. I follow my footprints back to the small *auberge.* Before going for dinner, I look at the dark sky, glittering with millions of stars.

I'm awake before the knock on my door. Last night I hired a guide and his camel to take me up the Erg Chebbi (the highest dune) to view the sunrise. I decline Achmed's offer to ride his camel. I'm more interested in photographing them in this big, sensuous landscape.

As we get farther into the desert, the sky begins to show some colour. I ask Achmed to walk on the crest of one of the dunes, camel in tow. I photograph them silhouetted against the sky. This could be a good selling image, and I take many photographs, altering their size within the picture space. I keep photographing after the sun has risen, now showing the desert bathed in warm hues. With the light still very pleasant, I ask my guide/model to lead his camel through the dunes while I photograph them walking away, as if disappearing into the unknown. It's been a good morning.

Back in Marrakech, I get up early so I can photograph as the city comes to life. From the Koutoubia mosque, I hear the call of the muezzin. The sun begins to cast long shadows, and I begin to take pictures. I'm close to one of the main gates inside the old city. As the heat increases, so does the bustle. I stand at a street corner and photograph the crowd entering the medina (old city), people walking or riding on bikes, mopeds or donkeys. An older man leads a horse-drawn carriage loaded with produce. Not far behind is a young man transporting no less than two hundred eggs on the back of his moped, an omelette waiting to happen. I'm very excited by what appears through my camera lens.

After breakfast, I get into *le petit taxi* and instruct the driver to take me to Le jardin Majorelle, named after the painter Jacques Majorelle and now owned by the famous couturier Yves Saint Laurent and his partner, Pierre Berge. At the entrance to this small oasis is a fountain decorated with tiles in shades of blue and green. This colour scheme is replicated throughout the garden, with the shades of green provided by the variety of plants, including palm trees, bamboo, aloes, cacti and water lilies. Cobalt blue is the colour of choice for the former villa — now hosting a small Islamic museum — the fountains and rills and many of the large clay pots scattered along the paths of the garden. A few pots painted in bright yellow and green accent this small Eden, a haven from the noise and heat of Marrakech.

Having obtained permission from the owners, I spend the morning photographing. Near the villa, one of the caretakers has just finished washing the floor, leaving it wet. In it is reflected a blue urn holding a pink bougainvillea. I must hurry as the sun is fast drying the shiny surface.

I walk over to a large pond filled with water lilies. The reflection of the villa in the water provides a surface of cobalt blue on which the flowers appear to be floating. Back to the villa: two windows with wrought-iron designs painted the brightest yellow are framed by a large intertwined vine. Beneath them, a bench and a large pot with flowers complete the setting. The garden closes for a few hours at noon; I leave, reluctantly.

I spend the afternoon walking through the souks of the *medina,* where shops line crowded, labyrinthine alleyways. I reject the offers of locals who want to be my guide. I prefer to wander on my own, knowing I'll most likely get lost. Fez pottery with blue paint set in geometric designs over white catches my eyes. Some of the plates and bowls inlaid with metal are very attractive and are meant as decorative pieces. I spot a set of bowls with black over white designs similar to those of henna tattoos, and make my first purchase.

Venturing on, I end up in a small square, Rahba Kedima, which lures me in with strange offerings such as potions for spells, dried lizards and live chameleons. Some woman are selling the Muslim hats (*copa*), and the price keeps coming down as I walk away. I stop to look at one of the *copas,* and end up buying ten.

Every shopkeeper wants to show me his wares. When I keep going, they say *"Seulement pour le plaisir des yeux!"* Babouches, lamps, spices, leather belts and bags, carpets and more carpets.

I stop for a bit of a rest and watch the daily rituals unfold in front of me. A man dressed in festive clothes and carrying a hawk is posing for tourists. I see in profile an older man in front of his shop. I set up to photograph him from afar but don't have the nerve to do it. Feeling watched, I decide to go over and ask permission to photograph him. He agrees and poses for me. I kindly ask him to look away. A profile is the photograph I intended to take. He offers mint tea, and I join him in his shop.

I find my way to Souk Smarine, the main artery, and head back to my hotel to drop off my purchases and get ready for the evening.

In the distance, I can hear the snake charmers' flutes as I head towards the Place Jma El Fna, the liveliest place in Marrakech, or in Morocco, for that matter. It is now five o'clock, and the main square is just beginning to buzz with locals and tourists. I'm a prime target for the performers, who notice my camera with its unusually large lens (a 100–400 Canon image stabilizer). Most offer their poses for a few *dirhams.* The sun is still a bit too strong, so I just walk around, scouting out the area and choosing whom I'd like to photograph later on. The snake charmers will be first, as they're sitting and will be the first to be shaded by the crowds that gather around them. Then I've decided on a group of colourful and attractive dancers. I need a good shot of the water sellers with their wild costumes and crazy hats, copper cups dangling around their necks. It's no wonder they make more money posing for tourists than they do selling water.

When the light is just right, I begin to shoot. I'm standing next to a man who is watching the crowd. He's wearing a cream-coloured *jelabba* embroidered with gold-hued fabric, and a *copa* covers his shaved head. Thick black-rimmed glasses conceal his eyes. At about fifteen feet from him, I point my camera right in his face and begin to photograph. He looks straight at me then looks back into the distance. A rush of excitement comes over me. I'm not usually this bold when photographing strangers.

I walk over to the snake charmers and begin to photograph them. I take a few shots of a tormented cobra, then include the charmer in the photographs. Some of the people watching us obscure the sun, and I keep having to push them sideways. One of the performers puts snakes around his neck and begins to pose. Because he's standing tall, the sun shines beautifully into his eyes. I tip them generously and move on to the dancers.

"Je veut plusieurs photos de vous tous." I make sure the leader of the group of dancers understands I'll be taking many photographs. We agree on a sum of money, and I proceed to photograph them as a group as well as shooting individual portraits. As more tourists appear with their small digital cameras, the dancers lose interest in me, seemingly forgetting how much money I paid them.

Young girls offer to tattoo my hands in henna, and the water sellers who see my camera try to coax me to photograph them. I notice a crowd surrounding some acrobats: they are attracting a lot of attention. As I walk towards them, I see a *stahl* where some cooks are preparing food for the evening. Wearing white, these men are engulfed by the backlit smoke rising from the acetylene. I anxiously take a few shots. Within minutes the smoke thins and the light is gone. I can only hope that I captured it on film.

With the light gone, I have lost my chance to photograph the acrobats. I retire to Place de l'Etoile, a café with a terrace overlooking the square. I order mint tea and, using my tripod, take a few last shots. There is still some ambient light in the sky. Combined with the artificial lights of the many food *stahls,* it should make for interesting photographs.

When evening falls, claiming the last bit of light, I put my camera away and drink my tea. I think to myself, what better place to end my trip? As I sit there watching the scene below, more stories will be told, many hands will be covered with henna, and the music will play on.

Opposite: Cooking at Place Jma El Fna, Marrakech.

Above: Berber brooch painted with henna on leather.

Opposite: Achmed and his camel on the dunes of Erg Chebbi, in the Sahara.

Intimate details of Le jardin Majorelle. Top left: Fountain in the cactus garden. Top right: Water lilies in a large pond. Bottom left: Hibiscus against a cobalt blue wall. Bottom right: Windows with vines and foliage.

Large agave plant in front of the Islamic museum at Le jardin Majorelle.

Portrait of a musician from the Atlas mountains.

Profile of an elder in the souks of Marrakech.

Place Jma El Fna. Top left: Water seller in colourful attire. Top right: Carpet detail.
Bottom left: Tea kettle. Bottom right: Musician.

Snake charmer, Place Jma El Fna.

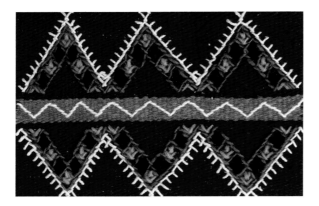

Above: Detail of a woven carpet.

Opposite: Panned photograph of a young man on a bicycle with eggs, Marrakech.

Following pages: The spectacular Draa valley.

Top left: Colourful pottery in a Marrakech souk. Top right: Window detail, Oumesnat.
Bottom left: Window and palm shadow, Marrakech. Bottom right: Carpets hanging on store wall, Essaouira.

Opposite: Brahim pouring tea, Tafraoute.

Above: Cooks getting ready for the evening, Place Jma El Fna.

Opposite: An evening at bustling Place Jma El Fna.

IDYLL PLEASURES

Above: Chairs on a beach with a stormy sky, Tortuga Beach, Grand Cayman Island. Opposite: Dramatic sky above tall ship, Grand Cayman Island.

I'm not a sun worshiper, and I don't care for sandy beaches. What draws me to the Caribbean is the aqua-hued water and the people who live there. I took several trips to the islands when I was working on my portfolio. In the winter months, I escaped to Barbados, Jamaica, the Dominican Republic, Margarita Island (Venezuela) and St. Martin, looking for images that would impress an art director enough to give me a chance. Later, I travelled twice to the Caribbean on assignment, once to Nevis for *Destinations* and once to Guadeloupe for an *En Route* story about how the people there celebrate Christmas. I've since continued my explorations, and have visited Aruba, Curaçao, the Bahamas, Grand Cayman and St. John. Here, I've assembled a collection of some of my favourite photographs. May "Idyll Pleasures" bring you a little bit of sunshine.

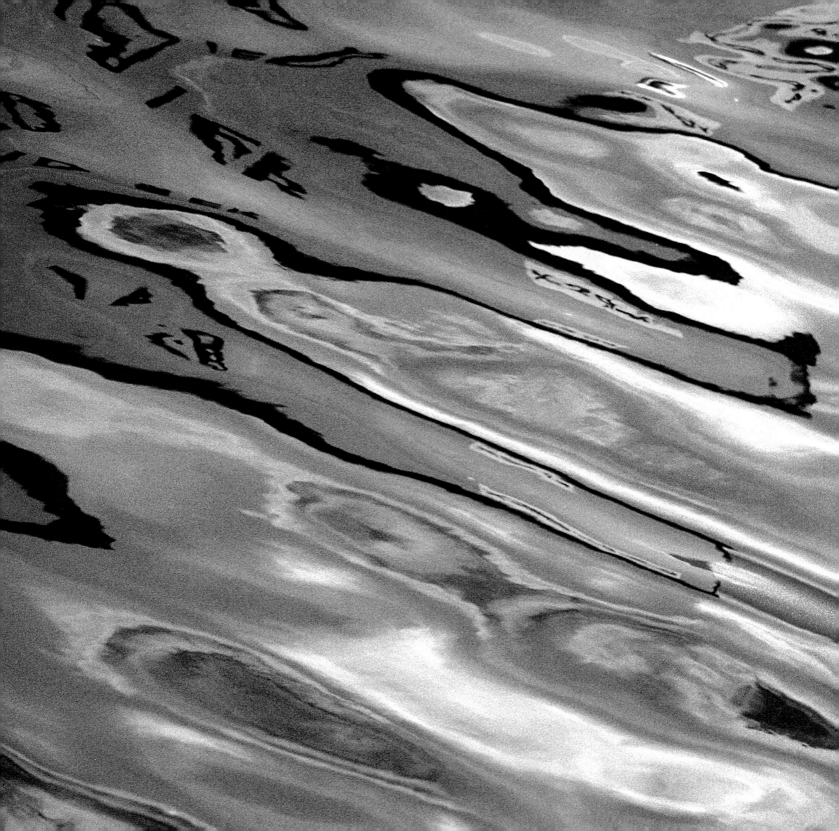

Top left: A stairway, St. Martin. Top right: Small lizard, Nevis. Bottom left: Hibiscus floating in pool, Dominican Republic. Bottom right: Another stairwell, St. Martin.

Opposite: Fishing boat reflection in the Caribbean Sea, Bridgetown, Barbados.

Top left: Pelican at rest on pillar, Aruba. Top right: Bougainvillea and its shadow near a yellow wall, St. Martin. Bottom left: Red hibiscus against a yellow wall, Aruba. Bottom right: Young boy (Peto) selling rum, Dominican Republic.

Opposite: Pelican in flight, Aruba.

Top left: Egret eating a lizard, St. Martin. Top right: Plant leaves, Dominican Republic. Bottom left: Lizard shadow on leaf, St. John. Bottom right: Waterfall (Chute du Carbet), Guadeloupe.

Opposite: Tropical forest, Parc National de la Guadeloupe.

Above: Scraping fish scales, Grand Cayman Island.

Opposite: Fishing boats, Six Men's Bay, Barbados.

Above: Portraits of schoolchildren, Montego Bay, Jamaica.

Opposite: Girls in uniform walk to school, St. Martin village, Barbados.

Above: Young boy playing in the sea with a toy boat, Margarita Island, Venezuela.

Opposite: Dramatic skies over a silver ocean, Nevis.

Above and opposite Sunset at Pinney's Beach, Nevis.

Above: Young woman with baby, Nevis.

Opposite: Man sitting in a doorway, Nevis.

Following pages: Windsurfing in Aruba.

When I lived in Toronto, I often travelled with my good friend Louise. I photographed her by the pool at the Crane Beach Hotel in Barbados (opposite), and in St. Martin I took a detail photograph of her hand holding a hat and a hibiscus flower (above).

SERENE CANVASES

Tulips, Scottish countryside.

I went through a phase in which I often used grainy colour slide film for travel photography. At the time, Agfa made a wonderful film, Chrome 1000. Warm in hue, the film, used under the right lighting conditions, produced beautiful, evocative images with high grain and subdued colours. The mood and softness was further enhanced by using a clear filter coated with hairspray in front of my lens. (Today, this grainy effect can easily be replicated using a program such as Photoshop. Select "Grain" under Filters, and you can add the desired amount of grain to your images.)

With this technique, I was able to convey visually how I felt about certain destinations: the romance of Venice, the serenity of the English countryside, the nostalgia of Scotland's castles. I eventually convinced a few art directors to let me use this film and filter combination on some of my travel assignments. When travelling to the U.K. "In Search of King Arthur," I felt the technique would be an appropriate way to depict the period of the story, and *En Route* agreed. Karen at *Destinations* also trusted my instincts when she assigned me to photograph "The Pilgrimage Route" in northwestern Spain's Galicia, where it usually rains two out of three days, a perfect lighting situation for this high-speed film.

"Serene Canvases" is a portfolio of some of my favourite images made using this film and technique.

Opposite: Bougainvillea, Costa Rican countryside

United Kingdom

Above: Stained glass at King Arthur's Great Halls, Tintagel.

Opposite: Grazing sheep in Somerset County.

Above: Swan near bridge, Great Wishford.

Opposite: Park benches in Wells.

Above: Crest on Dunster Castle, Dunster.

Opposite: Gold Hill, Shaftesbury.

Galicia, Spain

Above: Man with umbrella on the steps of Cathedral Santiago de Compostela.

Opposite: View of Santiago de Compostela.

Top left: Man in a dory, Malpica. Top right: Geraniums on windowsill, Malpica. Bottom left: Parked cars on a narrow street, Santiago de Compostela. Bottom right: Man in the small village of Malpica.

Opposite: Farming couple in the province of La Coruña.

Italy

Carnival masks in a window display, Venice.

Balcony with flowers, Burano.

Details of Venice. Top left: Gondola with reflections. Top right: Masks in a shop window. Bottom left: Colourful striped posts in the lagoon. Bottom right: Gondola ornament with reflections.

Opposite: View of Palladio's Church, off San Giorgio Maggiore, Venice.

Images of Burano. Top left: Cat in a colourful dory. Top right: Pot of flowers on a wall.
Bottom left: Pansies on a small balcony. Bottom right: Two white chairs in front of a house.

Opposite: Woman with her wash, Burano.

Above: Lamppost and gondolas on the lagoon, Venice.

Opposite: Lamppost and Santa Maria della Salute, a great Baroque church, Venice.

O CANADA

Wet maple leaves from my hometown, Edmundston, New Brunswick.

In 1994, Jack McIver, the founder and editor of *Destinations,* invited me to work on one of his projects. He wanted me to illustrate a book Pierre Berton would be writing, called *Winter.* Not much of a winter enthusiast, and inexperienced at photographing the bleak season, I welcomed the challenge, and felt the association with Pierre Berton would be an asset to my career.

I worked on the book during 1994 and 1995, traversing Canada from Newfoundland to British Columbia, with two trips north, one to the Yukon and one to the Northwest Territories, in search of evocative "winter" images. My work on the book helped me get to know my Canada, wearing white at this beautiful time of the year. It also introduced me to frozen fingers, frostbite on my face and the hazards of driving through blizzards.

Winter was a success, and it was followed by *The Great Lakes.* With Pierre Berton still at the helm, this time we included the United States in our text and photographs. I travelled around the five lakes — which often felt like oceans — at different times of the year, to capture the seasons and get variety in the photographs. In the summer of 1995, I experienced a heat wave in Chicago. For three days, soaked with sweat, I walked around the city's ethnic neighbourhoods, looking for images that would illustrate a section on the two big cities of the Great Lakes, Toronto and Chicago. A snowstorm later that year stranded me in a motel for three days in Owen Sound, Ontario, on Lake Huron.

Seacoasts was my last collaboration with Pierre, and I enjoyed my work on this book the most. I got to explore Canada's east and west coasts, as well as our great northern coast. I spent a week on a small ship, cruising parts of the Northwest Passage. On the west coast, I photographed the enchanting Queen Charlotte Islands, the Inside Passage, sections of Vancouver Island, including Victoria, and finally Vancouver. On the east coast, I drove around the Maritime provinces and travelled to Newfoundland and the small settlement of Nain, in Labrador. Finally, I visited two remote parts of the Northwest Territories, Inuvik and Tuktoyaktuk.

I remember shooting aerials through a small seaplane window as we flew over the Mackenzie Delta in Inuvik and the Tongat Mountains in Labrador. I flew in other small planes with my door removed, leaning out of the craft, trying to stabilize myself, as I aimed at the Confederation Bridge, which links New Brunswick to Prince Edward Island, and looked for a dramatic shot of the Campobello Lighthouse, silhouetted with backlight. This last one paid off: it graced the cover of *Seacoasts*.

With these three books, I became a better Canadian, acquiring knowledge, understanding and appreciation for my country. I also gained tremendous experience, great stories and memorable adventures. Thank you, Jack. Thank you, Pierre.

Here are a few special photographs from my Canada.

Children posing, Nain, Labrador.

Newfoundland

Above: Petty Harbour at dusk.

Opposite: Lighthouse at the entrance of St. John's.

Prince Edward Island

Above: P.E.I. resident (Catherine) serving lobster.

Opposite: Picket fence, houses and lighthouse in North Rustico.

Nova Scotia

Above: Small details of fishing shacks in West Pennant.

Opposite: Glorious morning light and reflection, Blue Rocks.

New Brunswick

Above: Fisherman with lantern, Acadian Peninsula.

Opposite: Fishing boats in harbour at dusk, Miscou Island.

Quebec

Top left: Canoe races on the Saint Lawrence River in wintertime. Top right: A peewee hockey game in Quebec City. Bottom left: Formula 1 snowmobile races in St. Gabriel de Brandon. Bottom right: Child with tire tube playing in the snow, Quebec City.

Opposite: View of Quebec City in the winter.

Ontario

The images above are of the wrought iron fence at Niagara Falls.

Opposite: Sun rising through the mist in February, Niagara Falls.

Manitoba

Above: Silhouette of cows and fence in the Manitoba prairie.

Opposite: Grain elevator at dusk.

Saskatchewan

Above: Herdsman with cattle on a cold morning in rural Saskatchewan.

Opposite: Snow-covered sheep near a small farm, Prince Albert.

Alberta

September crops near Cochrane.

Thick mist above silhouetted trees, Lake Louise.

British Columbia

Top left: Multiple exposure of spirit dance, Masset, Queen Charlotte Islands. Top right: Totem pole carving of eagle, Old Masset. Bottom left: Carved watchmen atop a totem pole, Skidegate, Queen Charlotte Islands. Bottom right: Portrait of a native carver, Duncan.

Opposite: Reg Davidson, a fine carver from Old Masset, performs the spirit dance on the coast of the Queen Charlotte Islands.

Yukon

Above: Street scene of Third Avenue in the snow at dusk, Dawson City.

Opposite: View of Dawson City and the river from the Midnight Dome above the city.

Northwest Territories

Top left: Kids playing in Pond Inlet. Top right: Snow prints and snowdrifts, Pond Inlet. Bottom left: Sled dogs awaiting a storm. Bottom right: Hands of a soapstone carver, Iqaluit.

Opposite: Man on a snowmobile next to an iceberg in a grand landscape northeast of Pond Inlet.

ABOUT TRAVEL PHOTOGRAPHY

Fishing on the Amalfi Coast, Italy.

There is more to travel photography than having a camera and lots of film. Good planning, preparation and research will help you maximize your photography time and will enable you to get the most from your travels. If you travel alone, with a partner or with friends, you'll have much more control over where you go and when you photograph than if you're with a tour. Ideally, try to surround yourself with people who have the same goal as you: to make pictures. They'll understand why you need to take time to set up your shots — they'll be doing the same! It's not fair to make non-photographers wait while you look for that winning shot; you'll just feel pressured to rush.

A photo tour is a good alternative. You'll be in the company of others who have the same goal. In such a group, it is understood that good morning light is more important than eating breakfast at a specific time. Then there are travel tours, with itineraries bursting at the seam. Six countries in Europe in three weeks!

The most you'll see is the inside of a bus. I was on a cruise of the Greek islands a long time ago, and we anchored near the island of Santorini. Our stop at this jewel island was all of two hours. To top it off, those two hours were from 11:00 a.m. to 1:00 p.m. Bad planning, both by the cruise line and by me. A lesson learned.

When getting ready for a trip, it's a good idea to plan and pack in advance. I don't particularly like lists, but with them, you're less likely to forget something that may cost much more abroad, or worse, that you won't be able to find. Here is a list of the essential photography equipment you'll want to bring. I keep this list on my computer and posted in my office.

- *Two camera bodies:* I usually alternate between two bodies every other day — in case one malfunctions, you'll still have half of your images.
- *Lenses:* I plan according to the type of trip. If the focus of my trip is people and street scenes, I'll bring two lenses: 24mm–70mm and 70mm–300mm. If I'm planning to shoot landscapes and scenery, I'll add a 17mm–35mm lens. If I'll be shooting wildlife, I'll pack my 100mm–400mm with a doubler. Bring only the lenses you're most likely to need. Too much equipment will weigh you down, and you'll become a bigger target for thieves.
- *Photo vest:* I like my equipment to be easily accessible, which is why I prefer a photo vest to a camera bag. And if someone is trying to steal my equipment, they'll have to get the vest off me first.
- *Film:* I always bring more film than I anticipate needing. Your film of choice may not be available at

your destination, and it's likely to cost twice as much. I average eight to ten rolls a day.

- *Digital equipment:* Bring camera bodies, memory cards with a lot of storage, a laptop and an electrical converter (depending on where you are travelling).
- *Filters:* A polarizing filter is very useful; I also like an 81A warming filter.
- *Batteries:* Always have extras, both in a camera bag and in your photo vest.
- *Camera flash:* Don't forget fresh batteries for your flash too!
- *Tripod:* When I fly, I pack my tripod in a hard suitcase, as they can easily be damaged in transit.
- *Reflector:* If I know I'll be photographing people, I pack a collapsible 48-inch reflector.
- *Notebook and pen:* These are important for writing down captioning information.

If you're travelling by air, pack wisely. Make sure to put all your film and equipment in your carry-on. Don't pack film in checked luggage, where it is most likely to get fogged by the X-ray machines. If you have the film with you, you might be able to have it hand-inspected by security. If the agents do not want to hand-inspect, it is safe to put film up to 800 ASA through the X-ray machine. In my twenty years of travelling, I've never had film ruined by X-rays.

PHOTOGRAPHING YOUR TRAVELS
When you get to your destination, photograph a variety of things, from people to scenics, making sure to include small details. If possible, plan to shoot at the

times of day that offer the best light. I like to get up early and be out an hour or so before sunrise. I photograph before the sun comes up — the cool light adds a nice mood to images. When the sun begins to shine, the light becomes warm, and the long shadows add impact to your photographs. Look for sidelight (to emphasize textures), and try using backlight for dramatic effect — but be careful of lens flare: if the sun is low, a lens shade won't be enough to shield the front of your lens, especially a wide lens. I like to rest at midday, when the light is harsh. I step out again, revitalized by a good rest, when the sun gets low in the sky.

Don't stop photographing just because the weather isn't great. You can get wonderfully moody images on wet and grey days. At these times I like to experiment with grainy film, getting results similar to the images in "Serene Canvases."

Don't overlook the details. They're one of my favourite things to photograph on my travels. They tell their own stories and add intimacy to travelogues.

Captioning and editing are very important parts of travel photography. I try to keep notes of what, when and where I photograph. I sometimes shoot signs with the names of villages, streets, churches, and so on after taking a series of photographs. It makes it easier when I label, edit and caption my slides weeks and sometimes months after returning home.

Scenics and landscapes can be very beautiful in and of themselves, but do not overlook the human element. A figure in a landscape adds interest and sometimes scale in a travel photograph. A silhouette can add a dimension of mystery. On my recent trip to India, I was photographing the Taj Mahal at sunrise. As beautiful as it was, the whole mood of the photograph changed when a man crossing the river appeared in my composition. Although very small in the scene, the silhouette adds impact to the image (see photo, pages 190–91).

PHOTOGRAPHING PEOPLE

When I'm travelling, I enjoy photographing people the most. A portrait, or perhaps a cityscape or street scene, can be more expressive of a place than a landscape. Looking back at my magazine covers, most had a person in them. There are two approaches to photographing people:

1) *The candid photograph.* These type of portraits can be difficult to take if you're timid and not used to this kind of photography. You have to be quick, ready and decisive. Good places to practise taking candids are markets, busy streets and parades. Wherever I travel, I'm always looking for colourful markets where I can shoot candids. On these occasions, I favour using a fast lens (80mm–200mm, f/2.8) rather than a tripod, which might make me stand out. I try to blend in with the crowd. Another approach is to find a vantage point where you can be unobtrusive but still see a lot of the activity. After a while, people ignore you, and you can make exciting photos as they go about their daily routines.

2) *The posed portrait.* Approach strangers with kindness and, if possible, engage them in conversation before asking to take their picture. I always introduce

Parading Oompah band, Bavaria, Germany.

myself and say where I'm from, why I've come to their country and why I want to photograph them. Digital cameras are a great ice breaker, because you can show your model what the pictures look like.

When you ask to photograph someone, you lose the spontaneity of a candid, but you have much more control. You can choose the direction of the light, you can select the background to some extent, and you can usually vary the expressions and poses of the person you're photographing. I always treat the people I pose

with the utmost respect. If there is a language barrier, I communicate with gestures, pointing to the camera, pointing to my smile if I want them to smile, pointing in the direction I'd like them to look. Remember, a smile goes a long way in these situations.

If a stranger has agreed to pose for me, I'll work fast to get a variety of images, shooting very tight close-ups and head-and-shoulder shots. If the surroundings are interesting, I'll add them to the picture, shooting more of an environmental portrait.

Aerial view of street from Hawa Mahal in Jaipur, India.

I'm often asked if I pay people to take their picture. I will "tip" a reasonable amount (between five and ten dollars) if I feel I can get some good images. I also always send photos to them if I promise to do so. It's sometimes a hassle, but I like to keep my word — and it makes it easier for the next photographer who comes along.

I usually carry model releases with me, but they seldom get signed unless I can clearly explain what a model release entails. This means I can't use the portraits for advertising or sell them through my stock agencies. Magazines with editorial content are now beginning to ask for model releases. It is the wave of the future.

Events such as festivals and parades are wonderful for taking both candids and posed portraits. Be bold — don't be afraid to aim your camera at people. These are also good opportunities to vary your shutter speeds and experiment with panning. With a slow shutter speed, looking through the viewfinder, follow your moving subject, click the shutter and keep the camera moving. This technique can create a beautiful effect, with your subject relatively sharp and with motion in the background (see, for example, the picture on pages 110–111 of the man with the eggs on the bike. It was shot at 1/15 of a second). You'll have to experiment with various shutter speeds, but here are some ideas on what to start with:

• people walking in parade: between 1 second and 1/4 of a second;

Deliberately blurred photograph (with the use of a slow shutter speed) of a young dancer in Cartagena, Colombia.

• child running: between 1/15 and 1/20 of a second;
• bicycle or moped: between 1/15 and 1/30 of a second.

The slower the shutter speed, the more motion and blurriness you'll create in the still background,

but your subject may well be less sharp at too slow a shutter speed.

Another of my favourite techniques to try at these events also uses a slow shutter to show motion. But this time, try to remain still (possibly by using a tripod or monopod) while you record the action. The blur of a moving parade or a dancer in costume can be very effective and will add motion, spontaneity and excitement to your photographs.

These two techniques can produce wonderful results, especially in low light.

My final word of advice is to use your camera as a tool to connect with people. On many occasions, strangers have allowed me to take a closer look into their lives because of my camera. A man I photographed in Portugal, who spoke a bit of English, asked me to come to his wine cellar to sample some of his wine, a cordial gesture on his behalf and a delightful experience for me. A woman in Jodhpur, India, insisted I photograph her children, and showed me into their home. When I left, her husband kindly gave me a package of curry. In Oaxaca, Mexico, after I had photographed an artist and his paintings, he invited me to have pizza with him and his mother at their place, where we shared good conversation, laughter and tears. These personal connections are the memories I cherish most from my many years of travelling.

Small silhouetted figure in front of the Taj Mahal, India.

THANK YOU...

Jack McIver of Zaxxis Publishing, for the great times at *Destinations*, and the Pierre Berton books.

Cate Cochran, the first to take a chance on me.

Karen Simpson, for all those wonderful assignments and your beautiful designs. You are the best.

Andrew Smith at PageWave Graphics, for all your help and good advice.

Sue Sumeraj, my editor, for encouraging me to express myself.

Dory in Blue Rocks, Nova Scotia.